PERMISSION TO FEEL LOVED

How to

Parents help

Teens

<u>develop</u>

Table of Contents

INTRODUCTION

A comprehensive study by Michelle Pham, a degree and master's degree holder in psychology from a great institution in Vietnam with 17 years of experience in educational management to date. She is a great thinker that believes in our minds and what we feed them make up who we are today. She takes her time to put down unique content to bring up good stories **"Permission to feel loved – How to Parents help teens develop"** to entertain and educate us. Thus, from birth, parents are among the essential people in children's lives. A teenager learns to trust their mother, father, and other caregivers to protect, care for, and care for them. Caring for and planning a course to promote general wellbeing. Although parents are often keen to learn more about their teenager's personality, many don't know how to take better care of themselves. Parenting is usually welcome, but in some cases, parents have difficulties and uncertainties about their ability to ensure their teenager's physical, emotional, or financial wellbeing.

At the same time, this study was primarily based on the understanding that ensuring the healthy development of teenager is not the sole responsibility of parents or families. It also lies with local, state and federal government as well as organizations that offer programs and services to support parents and families. Society has the social and economic support it needs for present and future generations to raise a healthy and wealthy teenager. In short, if parents and other caregivers can support young children, the lives of the teenager will be enriched, and their contribution will benefit society.

So that their children can have positive experiences, the parents immediately use the resources they know or have available. At best, these features can vary in quantity, availability, and quality, and at worst, they can be offered arbitrarily or in some way.

Resources can be close (e.g. family members) or distant (e.g. government programs). Access to them can be very expensive or inherently inadequate.

Regardless of early childhood programs, classrooms, children's clinics, or family networks, supporting children is key to improving healthy first childhood experiences, promoting positive outcomes for a teenager, and helping parents build close relationships with children.

TEENAGE – Chapter 1

Everyone knows that puberty is a difficult time for human growth and development. When the sudden flow of hormones causes physiological changes, the child prepares for reproduction. In some societies or cultures, the ability to reproduce identifies the person as an adult. It is not the case in the United States because the legal age is 18 years. Puberty is usually between 10 and 13 years old, this leaves a period of 5 to 8 years, and the parents are always responsible for the adult what we call adolescence.

Beginning Adolescence

Hormonal changes automatically generate the adult body and are beyond the control of the individual. The first suggestion is that the child grows. Since growing up is physical work, although adults don't see it that way, teenagers are tired of sleeping. The irony is that the body releases growth hormones during sleep, which makes the person tired. As all parents know, a bored child is humble and challenging. Even young people

Growth monitoring is the secondary indicator of sexual traits that we call puberty. Women begin menstruation, develop breasts and bumps. Men have arousal, their vocal cords thrive and start to sprout in the areas of the face.

For men and women, these are shocking and embarrassing changes that everyone with greater responsibility in school must agree on. Students change teachers and are not accountable to anyone during the school day. Teachers expect a higher level of independent work and responsibility to complete the activities. Activities take longer, which is difficult for teenagers with hormonal effects and a greater need for sleep.

Adolescence

Adolescence usually takes place at the beginning of puberty. They do not have an adequate "social filter" in their thinking process; the comments in which relationships develop often lead to a common disease of FMD and they have no idea what is causing the problem. Events often trigger emotional epidemics, the scope and duration of which are generally inadequate. Check out when adults give instructions or try to discipline themselves. Loud voices, profanity and insolence, are characterized by "conversations", followed by sulking, slamming doors or isolation in their rooms. The request for permission to go anywhere or do something usually ends with arguments that are interrupted "why not" or "everyone can / wants ..." when parents say "no". Older adolescents, usual men, can participate in physical confrontations or challenges with parent figures.

Adolescence is the developmental phase between childhood and adulthood, which is characterized by rapid changes in physical, psychosocial, moral and cognitive growth. There are three stages of adolescence: early (11-13 years), medium (14-16 years) and late (> 17 years). Each of these phases differs in terms of the development goals that your adolescent must achieve. We are all different, and not all children reach certain stages at the same time as other children. The most important thing is to support your children and to be patient within healthy limits and rules.

Think about these stages of development when you interact with your adolescent:

Independence

At the beginning of puberty, children want to separate from their parents. They prefer to spend more time with friends than with the family. In middle adolescence, children are not clear about the separation, but at the end of a teenager, the child has to solve these problems.

Body Image

In early adolescence, the boy adapts to changes in puberty. In the middle of a Teenager, children "experiment" with different images to find their true self. The child must develop a satisfactory body image at the end of puberty.

Relationship

In childhood, children are parents of unisex friends. In the middle of puberty, your son spends more time in a heterosexual group. At the end of adolescence, expect that individual relationship is more important for your child than for the peer group.

Career Plans

Career plans are vague in the first half of teenagers. When your child reaches puberty, there are individual goals and steps to take.

Value System

Your first Teenager will test your moral system. Young people in the environment are absorbed in themselves. Late adolescents have a strict idea of good and evil and are managed differently.

Sexual Drives

Early boys are sexually curious and can have sexual experiences until mid-puberty.

At the end of puberty, however, they begin with a close relationship and care.

Your child needs privacy at the beginning of puberty. It can be achieved by allowing the young person to have their bedroom. If you cannot provide it, your child should have a separate room in a discreet room.

Prepare for your young people to maintain their independence. Your adolescent has a sufficient psychological need to separate from you and establish his identity as an individual. For most teenagers, this is sure to be achieved through clothing, hair, jewelry, music, and the growing importance of close friends. Because young people are separated from their parents, they need the support of their colleagues to provide psychological protection (support structure) in which they can grow outside of the family. But that doesn't mean that you no longer love your child. You need more than you think, so let them know about your concerns (don't embarrass them in front of your friends!).

Depression in Adolescent

Depression is a mental disorder that can cause psychological and other symptoms. According to some studies, 5 to 8% of young people worldwide are affected by depression. Children are more prone to depression than teenagers. Depression symptoms in adolescents are challenging to identify, so they are usually not diagnosed.

However, the most common symptoms of depression in adolescents are:

1. Permanent sadness is the best-known symptom of depression in adolescents.

2. Irritability

3. One of the main characteristics is the feeling of worthlessness.

4. Sleep disorders, such as excessive sleep or insomnia.

5. Difficulties at school, such as concentration and less interest in extracurricular activities.

6. Problems with relatives and friends.

7. Less interested in daily activities.

8. Low self-esteem.

Teenage depression can be easily cured. You just have to recognize the symptoms of depression. It is essential to understand the symptoms and find a suitable treatment in good time so that the effects of depression in adolescents can be eliminated. The exact cause of adolescent depression is not yet known. Experimental studies have shown that it is a biological disorder due to the chemical imbalance of serotonin and dopamine in the brain. These chemicals are the leading causes of the normal functioning of the human mind, including sensation, movement, emotions and memory.

Most teenagers are not sure why they are depressed. You should understand that this is usually due to stress or emotional events in your environment. The most common causes of **depression in teenagers** are listed below.

1. It could be due to genes.

2. You may have had childhood depression.

3. Sudden death in family or friends or someone you love.

4. Adolescents are more likely to experience depression if they have ever had anxiety or ADHD (Attention Deficit Hyperactivity Disorder).

5. Family problems such as conflicts between home and father.

6. The complicated inferiority of other teenage friends at school.

7. Negative thinking about the most beautiful things.

The effects of depression on teenagers can be very destructive. You may have difficulty going to school regularly, homework problems, and parents. Other issues that adolescents can have are health problems such as the upset stomach, loss of energy or fatigue, and headache. You can also treat smoking, alcohol, drugs, etc. Suicidal tendencies can also develop in the minds of young people. Adolescents must seek appropriate treatment because the harmful effects of depression can affect their future. There are many treatment modalities, such as medication, psychological therapies, energy therapy, etc. You just need to consult the specialist and carry out the prescribed treatment.

PARENTHOOD – Chapter 2

Parenting is a profession that deserves the planning and hard work of paid work. People grow a lot more in their careers than in their careers. Parenting offers the opportunity to broaden your perspective as parents try to shape the traits; they want their children to see. For some parents, raising their children is the chance to be the parents they want.

Parenthood as a Growth Process

Parenthood requires sacrificing personal interests in terms of career, fun, and entertainment. It means loss of privacy, time and own freedom. It causes emotional, physical, financial stress, concerns about children's health, behavior, and performance.

It includes disruptive behaviors, noise, and distractions. Pregnancy and childbirth have physical and health consequences for women.

With all these disadvantages, it is surprising that parents attract everyone. For most people, birth and education are highly creative processes that satisfy their biological skills in reproduction and care. Biological and adoptive children offer parents growth opportunities by transferring their childhood and caring for adults. In the process of mutual growth, child-rearing is the exchange of ideas, feelings and power when children and parents learn to respect and influence each other.

Unfortunately, parenting is often not seen as an opportunity for personal growth and discovery. As a result, many parents live in families more than just family members who live separate lives. Since the seduction of materialism and individualism promotes the pursuit of personal excellence and the purchase of things, many parents and children are not used as a source of joy and affirmation. These parents do not recognize their growth potential in family life.

❖ **<u>Strong Family</u>**

More research has been done on disturbed and disturbed families than on healthy families. However, essential studies show that competent parenting is a protective factor that avoids social problems and a decisive factor in promoting a successful life.

Developmental psychologists Hamilton McCubbin and Charles Figley describe a study of parenting skills in "strong families". A healthy family was defined as a family of mutual respect between family members who always had positive views about life, expressed through open affection and open communication. In these families, individuals had an explicit value for who they were and not for what they had achieved. The family members had realistic expectations, so the children learned what was acceptable and what was not, and allowed parents and children to correct their mistakes. The parents gave clear instructions and set reasonable limits, emphasizing the positive rather than the negative.

In healthy families, family growth is an experience for parents and children. Parents do not fully participate in their children's lives. They have precise moral meanings that are expressed through their words and actions. They have meaning and purpose in life, often accompanied by spiritual advice and a confident and optimistic outlook on life. They treat their children with courtesy and respect. By experiencing irrationality, family members can relax, "shake their hair", and refuel to meet the rational and irrational demands they make in a world outside of the home. Parents and children, in particular, recognize their mistakes. You can forgive.

Healthy family members follow family traditions and routines. Also, share power, and decision making among their members. They express their feelings, concerns and interests, listen and react to what others are saying. Their communication styles are bright, and people are encouraged to take responsibility for their feelings, thoughts and actions. They spend time together, but they value individual privacy and pursue independent interests.

Healthy families are also involved in the world in which they live. They show solidarity with each other and with others outside of their families. A healthy family contributes to the development of its members and the well-being of its community and society. Members of a healthy family have lasting relationships.

The legitimate use of parental violence is at the heart of healthy families.

❖ <u>Parental Authority</u>

In contrast to the old family, church and state orders, American culture has moved away from the dominant image of the father. The image of the American Revolution, which rejects the authority of the British king, is reflected in today's extreme sensitivity to abuse of power and even undermines the legitimate authority of parents in American families.

Because of this anti-authority ethic, many parents are unaware that freedom only makes sense in connection with legal restrictions, so that personal freedom does not restrict others' freedom. We cannot avoid the effects of our democracy on others. For this reason, all groups that work successfully have legitimate permissions. This authority is based on the knowledge, wisdom and experience that group members value. In families, these characteristics are generally felt by the parents.

The exercise of legitimate parental authority is based on two primary principles. The first is to understand that children are individuals with health needs and feelings from birth. The second is to create a productive life for children who are influenced more by their parents than they say. When parents control the effects, their children learn to behave civilly and deal with the inevitable frustrations of life. When parents delay satisfaction, the children learn to plan pleasant and unpleasant activities. Learn the ingredients for a productive life. When parents impede achievement, the children learn to plan pleasant and unpleasant events. Learn the elements for a productive life.

The bonds between parents and children form the basis for romantic relationships with others in adulthood. Parents who are involved in their children's behavior help them develop respect for others. They also learn to postpone satisfaction and suffer from the frustration of their years and desires. By trusting in future visions, children learn to overcome the obstacles in their daily lives. You are also encouraged to make the world a better place to live in. All of this is respected by an atmosphere of parental authority.

Thus, Parental authority is exercised through the creative use of power, ethics, family priorities, the affirmation of children, and family participation in their community and society.

❖ <u>The Creative Use of Power</u>

The word power is derived from the Latin Poder and means "To be Able". Everyone must be able to understand their strength. At the center of personal power is the feeling of being responsible for our lives. By taking responsibility for ourselves and our behavior, we acquire our power.

Both sides of parental love show enough affection and care to help the child learn self-discipline. Although the negative behavior of young children is frustrating for everyone involved in caring for them, it is a sign of their growing freedom. At the same time, their behavior requires a corresponding threshold adjustment. They also need models of parental self-discipline to learn, tolerate frustration, and delay the satisfaction of their effects.

Parental violence is appropriate when parents gradually give up their children's power. The goal is to creatively share power among family members, not under their control. Unlike independent parents, competent parents share strength by helping their children find their talents and deciding what to do with their lives. The legitimate exercise of power is not the same as victimization when parents and children have difficulty controlling themselves.

In childhood, there are times when a parent is responsible for a child and other times when a child is responsible for a parent. The challenge for parents is to learn how to switch between management and succession roles with their children properly. For example, a small child has excellent power and leads the parents, which changes the cycle of eating and sleeping. To do this, parents must respect and trust a child and generally respect and trust them.

Parental control of the border agreement is shown below. Many parents don't understand how important it is to set limits for young children. Your requests are easy to deliver. The hardest but most satisfying course is to help them learn the limits of their power. At this point they appear before the ability to think, it is necessary to communicate in the form of a non-physical deviation to respect the child, the parents determine the correct use of the word "no".

Most children, of course, check the limits and find out what is available. They quickly testify against their brothers and sisters and their colleagues. They desire what they want when they want it. It means that parents are asked to set clear boundaries and to show children that parents want to say what they say. In other to translate this into physical deviation and reluctance of the child, it must be demonstrated that the words of the parents must be taken seriously. Verbal commands in the room are easily ignored so that a child can go out so that what the parents say does not have to be taken seriously. The most effective way to convey this message to children is to intervene directly on their feet and hands and not walk around the room with their voices.

Similarly, the message is that these behaviors can be used to manipulate adults if the easiest way to alleviate discomfort or tantrums is chosen. A crying or controlling child should be placed in an environment where they can regain control without unduly affecting family life. When the child returns to his parents when he is ready, the message is that the time limit is to regain self-control, not disciplining.

❖ <u>The Practice of Morality</u>

If we like it or not, "good" and "bad" are the real polarities in life. This polarity has been the basis of philosophy for centuries. For small children, "good" and "bad" are the only essential value judgments.

The word "bad" is inappropriate if the children do not respect the wishes or expectations of the parents and exercise their autonomy in the event of non-compliance. "Bad" should be reserved for general and disloyal behavior towards others. They are dealing with family problems with "good", and "bad" can be treated more meaningfully with "bad" and "good".

"Right" and "wrong" depend on the judge's point of view. The ancient Greeks asked this question because Plato's observation shows that killing a lamb was good for humans but bad for wolves.

Children can distinguish right from wrong and to be generous, compassionate and selfless. They are expected to take care of and react to the emotional state of others, which is easy to recognize in the early stages of life. Familial ties and patterns reinforce these orientations. They wither when they are not connected to others. Children receive values, fashion and prosocial or anti-social interests from their peers, teachers, religions, films, literature and television.

"Good" (right) and "bad" (wrong) can be divided into manageable parts. Good things are about truth (trust in reality) and love (giving to others). The primary themes of forgiveness are emotional honesty (taking responsibility for your feelings and actions) and creative use of power (constructive influence on others). Evil deception (a change in confidence in reality) and harm to others (guilt) are a setback.

The irrational aspects of family life offer children and parents many opportunities to learn to express and deal with the "good" and the "bad". Most family conflicts affect parents and children who are wrong or hurt each other and therefore offer the opportunity to learn to take responsibility for their feelings and actions and to deal constructively with the effects on others. Hurt and cheated.

The distinction between "good" and "bad" in family life in terms of justice leads to interactions between parents and children for moral reasons and not to arbitrary definitions of good and evil based on the convenience or wishes of the parents. It introduces justice to the upbringing of children and not to the simple exercise of parental authority. For example, children can be expected to learn from others because respecting others' rights is a moral benefit and not because parents are irritated when they are not.

A healthy family is a family that has mutual respect and is not strongly influenced by their personal needs or desires. However, families cannot always be "just" communities. The guidelines on how to tell the truth or not interrupt when others speak are often unfair to parents and children. Parents look forward to a degree of privacy that they don't give our children. As a rule, a family member should be committed most of the time or wrongly accused of having started confrontations between brothers and sisters. The best efforts to establish impartiality in a family cannot be entirely successful because a family is an imperfect organization made up of imperfect creatures. Therefore, family life, as is all life, is a struggle between good and evil and the struggle for justice. The questions ask parents to clarify their moral values and encourage them to become stronger.

Family is the perfect test for overcoming your weaknesses, slowly losing patience and becoming fast. Understand when it's activated; try not to surprise others with your importance; Think of the best, not the worst. And don't be satisfied with the mistakes and failures of others. Most errors in family life due to selfishness, jealousy and irrationality instead of "wrong" actions or omissions are harmless omissions and judgments.

Because family ties are so intense, family members' mistakes can be the most difficult to forgive. At the same time, it is the place where forgiveness is most needed and wanted because it is impossible to hide human fault in a family.

❖ Family Priorities

Parental violence includes defining family priorities for motherhood, fatherhood, housework, career, stress management, and family routines.

Because parents have to bear the costs paid by adults without children, parents have to anticipate the financial consequences that increase with the age of their children. A fair balance has to be struck between educational, economic and professional goals. Everything in life can rarely be accomplished at the same time.

Careful management of family income and time based on family values and goals is becoming increasingly urgent.

It involves:

➢ family financial planning,
➢ Care in purchasing to assure value received.
➢ ongoing care of living and personal needs,
➢ Deliberate use of time for private, family and community events and commitments.
➢ Adequate nutrition and medical care.

Above all, financial goals must be managed where material things have a lower priority than the time they spend with the family. In the years that followed, many parents wanted to spend more time with their children and earn less.

Family stress can be minimized by planning family time for relaxation, recreation and fun. It includes designing the childless time for the parents. Otherwise, newspapers, television, and computers only give parents and children a few free minutes to have fun.

Family management includes programmable planning activities such as traditions, festivals and routines. Traditions like Thanksgiving and Christmas are holidays. Celebrations are special events that highlight the present, such as birthdays and anniversaries. Habits are regular daily and weekly activities.

A useful principle for maintaining household routines is that each family member is responsible for doing as much as possible for the good of the family.

Parental Affirmation

The inner mental images of our parents and other influential people are central elements of our personality.

We all grow up with a series of inner "good" and "bad" images that have family interactions with our parents and siblings in our lives today. These pictures are the "inner family" that stays with us for a lifetime. These intimate images appear to be "beyond your shoulders" and affect current interactions. They can react if they cause unresolved conflicts in our youth. As parents, we take pictures of our children's inner families.

For these reasons, children need to develop "good inner images" that result from parents confirming their maturity in the hope that they will achieve the highest level of puberty that their children are capable of. Children need confirmation of their individuality and competence right from the start. Parents, in turn, are confirmed when their children become competent and responsible people later in life.

Learn to express your thoughts and feelings verbally.

Affirmation in family relationships is based on open communication so that parents and children understand each other's thoughts, feelings and needs. This communication depends on listening, expressing thoughts and feelings and mutual understanding.

Children, in particular, need to learn from their parents how to find words to share their feelings with others. They tend to live their feelings instead of expressing them in words. Parents can shape communication by verbally expressing their emotions rather than just responding to them. For example, if you explain that a parent has a headache, the child can better understand the angry mood of the parent than angry words.

When children learn to express their feelings with words rather than actions, they gain confidence. Otherwise, they ineffectively resolve their tensions into emotional outbursts. Misunderstandings due to incorrect verbal communication are the basis of most family conflicts.

The way we deal with our emotional reactions to others is our responsibility. We can fight emotionally or use words to express our feelings. The most useful answer when others hurt our feelings is to say that our emotion is hurt honestly. We are best served when we share our verbal beliefs with others instead of reacting blindly.

The way parents deal with their problems sets an example for their children. The controversy still contests the brothers and sisters over the holiness of the parents. Separating them until they are "cold" is generally more effective than taking sides. Despite the emphasis on sibling rivalry, most sibling relationships have been fun over the years. Children, but they feel loyal to their brothers together and see them as good and not better. Friends.

When parents and children can verbally communicate their feelings and needs, blind emotional outbursts are minimized. You can put yourself in the position of the other person. It promotes empathy in children.

Building Self- Esteem by Affirming Individuality

Each child's declaration of individuality promotes the development of their self-esteem. A child's self-esteem test increases parents' self-esteem.

The explanation differs from the approval because the application for approval can keep the children waiting and deprive them of their individuality and the confirmation by the children increases their personality. Parental insurance aims to strengthen a child's self-esteem. Based on this certification, there is an additional need for approval and contempt for children to learn to recognize and regulate the effects of their behavior on others.

A child's statement begins by showing a child's innate strength in childhood by mimicking eye contact and sounds. This improvement in the child's spontaneous expression promotes real child development rather than self-imitation. If a parent does not react to a child's actions but replaces them, imitation is encouraged rather than individuality. Parents also later confirm that they touch, kiss, hug, fight, and play with their children. Younger children who are not connected in this way can ultimately find it attractive and uncomfortable.

Building Self-Esteem by Affirming Personal Competence

It strengthens not only the child's competence but also the child's self-esteem.

Part of happiness is incredible happiness. They are not "funny" in fun or fun activities. Feel with you and the world at the same time. It is a subjective feeling of wellbeing and satisfaction, and its intensity varies from person to person. It reflected in the self-esteem that results from early childhood experiences that have a high impact on the body and can be useful in the world. His prototype is to smile at a child in the first phase of the walk. Self-esteem is an internal measure of personal competence.

Self-esteem is strengthened by using language as a guide for our actions. As a means of thinking and communicating, communication improves problem-solving, learns from the consequences of one's actions, builds meaningful relationships with others and plans for the long term. When thoughts accompany activities, there should be no conflict between our basic instincts and our self-esteem. The self-esteem that results from personal competency that comes from eliminating our innate implications is less than integrating our legitimate interests into reflective research.

To promote self-esteem, parents need to ensure that their children know that their love does not depend on their behaviour. Therefore, it is better to look at children who are "bad" or "good" than "bad" or "good";

Help children avoid repeating the same mistake instead of criticizing them for making a mistake. Accept children as they are instead of comparing them to other children. Avoid speaking to children as if they weren't there. And be aware of children's sensitivity to appearance and avoid nicknames.

Children need boundaries, but how they are treated determines what they learn. For example, if children's behavior is unacceptable, you can first ask them if they understand why their behaviour is unacceptable. So you can ask what could help you avoid this behavior in the future. It transfers responsibility for self-control to the child. If a parent trusts the child's ability to improve, the child's self-esteem develops.

A feeling of competence is encouraged by parents who encourage them to present themselves to the risks and assume their responsibilities, which makes them happy. They then confirmed to their children that they tried new things, even if they failed. It encourages you to go for it rather than avoiding the risks. There is a point of intersection where fear is felt, contrasted and used as a source of warning and energy. If we can have children responsible for the consequences of their actions, we need to learn much more about the price of risk than on any outdoor trip to the desert.

Learning to manage mistakes is at the heart of learning to take risks. For adolescents, school work and risky extracurricular activities, such as sports, maybe a better factor of security than paid work. Earning money can only create a sense of responsibility for young people, but it can promote self-centered material if the payment is not used to buy luxury items.

The most important goal for parents and children is to find peace within themselves. For this reason, you are considered competent; children should develop a clear understanding of their activities and responsibilities. You have to learn to tolerate frustration and postpone satisfaction. You must be happy to love others. They don't concern you.

If we respect each other, we don't have to belittle others to get up. The awareness of our imperfect being enables us to accept the imperfections of others. In this way, the search for power over others can be replaced by affirmation of others through wealth, physical strength, weapons and criticism.

Family Participation in its Community and Society

Families are empowered through participation in their communities, as well as social and environmental problems. Families are the foundation of their community and society. These are fundamental elements of the ecosystem in which we all live. The idealism of children and adolescents can be promoted by inclusion in social and ecological questions and at the same time by distorting reality.

The responsibility of people to take care of their family and the country can be a central issue in family life. Family discussions and activities can focus on participating in a community, national, and global issues related to peace and land protection. In this way, the family can be a source of support for the creative life of the community and reconciliation. This type of active participation in their communities helps young people to reduce the fear of the future.

Families can also play a key role in suggesting and designing alternatives to violence to solve problems. In this way, they can participate in movements that oppose injustice and promote peace. Help children understand that poverty and oppression can make people feel helpless and hopeless, which in turn leads to violence. They can help link the violence they experience in their lives to violence around the world. They can be encouraged to become peacemakers in their region and thereby develop a world vision for peace.

PARENT'S EDUCATIONAL RESPONSIBILITY

Although school education is vital to our children's wellbeing, and they learn the basics of academics at school, as parents, we have ultimate responsibility for educating our children as a world. It is our right to teach our children morality, ethics and values.

Although two people on the planet don't have the same answers to many life dilemmas, we can only give one example. Our education, experience and training will play an essential role in what we teach our children and what they learn from us through observation and example. I know we all want the best for our kids, we want them to be happy, have a career they love, a couple who love them as much as we do and who have a good life. And what do we teach them about life that will ultimately protect them better from the needs that will undoubtedly bring them and will show respect and appreciation for their blessings?

I tried to teach my daughters to have a loving heart and to be kind to all living things. I also taught them to fight, to kick someone who intentionally hurts, be it physical, verbal or emotional, and to help a less fortunate man. You know the basics. ;-) "Do something for others" is a slogan that you should follow. I don't know of any religion or philosophy that contradicts this primary truth.

Remember that our children see all of our movements and use the hours of life as the last role model for what life throws at us. If we have a terrible day and decide that kicking the dog is an excellent way to relieve stress, our children will learn that it is okay to mistreat small animals and therefore someone or something else is no less powerful or less to learn. Abuse heavily. If we accept a bad day and ask for a hug, a little understanding and peace, they will learn that the desire to meet their needs is as valid as the needs of others and bad days are happening. But the way we treat them is critical.

Teaching our children to love each other is an essential step in this process. If you spend your life respecting yourself and not letting others compromise your wellbeing, you have a crucial weapon in your composition to overcome life's obstacles. It does not mean that we should teach our children to deny the feelings or wellbeing of others, or that they are mighty and superior to everyone else. It should show them that mutual respect and respect are an integral part of the game. Showing love and respect for your children will help them feel friendly and respectful.

We are also the guardians of our children's intellectual and philosophical state. They are parents who give children spiritual principles like any church or religious advice. If we reject this responsibility, our children learn the spiritual identity of others because spiritual beliefs are a convenient search in life. Spiritual beliefs should not be strict practices or dogmas issued by a church or organized religion. They can be any rule and value by which you can live and make decisions.

Children generally have no different ideas about life and the meaning of life. They are conditioned by parents and families and exposed to these principles. You will also learn to think about life and challenge the esoteric ideas of experience. If one day our teen arrives with a shaved head and terrible tattoos on his body because he entered a different culture or group that convinces our son that this is the path of salvation, immortality, or some other philosophical ideal. Whose fault is it? If we expose our child to our spiritual or philosophical practices and beliefs, they will likely consider these beliefs to be ugly truths, and we do not need to look for answers elsewhere, perhaps less than we want to. In essence, we build our baby's foundations when these times of destruction occur and develop strong roots to support them in times of crisis and confusion.

What Other **Important** Lessons Can We Teach Our Children?

Think about how we treat our parents. With kindness and empathy, your children will learn to manage you immediately. If you treat the homeless in the market with contempt and bigotry, your children will learn to handle the homeless and other less happy people without compassion.

We are the best examples of our children's lives. If you respect the kindness and kindness of others, you are likely to raise kind and kind children. If you appreciate the intelligence and financial responsibility, you are to teach your child these traits that are brilliant and financially responsible, because "that's what we do".

If we teach our teenager to see the world positively and kindly, they will have an essential weapon in their form to overcome the obstacles in life. If we show our teenager that life is unfair and cruel and that the challenges are hopeless, they will learn to see negativity and pain in daily challenges instead of believing that they are the ones who make life positive and meaningful. You can win and be happy instead of being afraid.

There are so many lessons that we teach our children. Take this responsibility seriously and consider who your children should be. It can be particularly crucial for children who grow up under less than ideal circumstances. Think of the stories of many ideals in our world some come from financially unstable and far from perfect houses. They often have the stories of parents or grandparents who took responsibility for that child seriously and promoted high self-esteem, morals and values to help that person succeed today.

EDUCATIONAL SUPPORT – Chapter 3

The story of Mandy Mandy, 17, praised by her case manager for her work and income, is in my office at Young Parents College. The four-week-old son sleeps next to her in the stroller. I try to get her in, offer her a cup of hot Milo and respect her little Akiwa. She is concerned about this new unknown environment and has some preliminary questions: "How are the other girls?" Are you friendly? "I promise you that at some point everyone was new to college and felt shy and insecure, but it was a very welcoming place and unlike the" regular "school. Teachers say their names, and we do a lot of interesting activities and excursions, in addition to that "Normal" homework. Children love to babysit and make lots of friends. "I don't like school," she said. "I went to my 10th grade." What have you done since then? I ask. "I worked in the supermarket, became pregnant and had to leave when I was away for seven months. Most of the time, I was exhausted and couldn't checkout. "Why do you still need it? Are you coming to school "I don't have a degree, you know, and I want something better for Akiwa? I want to get my NCEA and have a good job and a good salary so I can give him a better life than him. I don't want to "Mandy is a composite production that comes from talking to several hundred teenage mothers over fifteen years. I met many young women like Mandy when they went to a teen school to talk about their registration. "Mandy" was concerned when she was attending Teen Parent School because of her negative experiences with regular school. She thought she was a student with limited ability; she had primarily rejected high school and "dropped out" without having finished school. Mandy had no personal trust, and like many young women I have worked with, she was afraid to meet other girls at school. Like many teenage parents, Mandy was already working (in unskilled jobs) when she became pregnant, and her pregnancy was the driving force behind her perspective on changing the value and importance of education. Her long-term goal was to find a "good job" to make "Akiwa" a better life than ever.

If you are a teenager or a pregnant mother, you are still entitled to the same education and training as other students. While exercise can be challenging for you, knowing your options and the way forward is possible.

Schools are legally obliged to support young parents and pregnant adolescents in their studies. Schools may need to adjust the way they teach, the way they rate it, the uniform or dress code, and even the hours required to ensure that their education continues.

A limited number of secondary schools offer childcare or support services to pregnant adolescents and parents. Talk to a communal worker, counsellor, or your (prenatal) health team to find out which schools are helping young parents.

If you feel discriminated against or bullied at school, speak to someone you trust, e.g. a counsellor, a young worker, or another school worker.

Other Education Options

If you prefer not to go to a regular school, you have a choice of other options, for example.

- **<u>Distance learning</u>:** Enables learning at home, usually via registration and online access.
- **<u>Alternative educational centers that can provide support on campus</u>**, e.g. Childcare or a designated area where parents can study, relax or feed their children
- **<u>Universities such as TAFE</u>**, which offer training and further education in various sectors.
- **<u>Home Lessons</u>:** In this case, your parents receive personalized instruction and are responsible for planning the practice, including conducting learning activities,

organizing assessments, and monitoring progress.

+ **<u>Open College:</u>** Offers distance learning for nationally recognized and industry-recognized courses that support students through an online learning portal where they can interact with each other and with their trainers.

+ **<u>Other programs:</u>** Some schools offer unique programs to help pregnant students or parents.

Education is the key. Whichever option you choose, as long as it suits you.

TIPS:

There is no doubt that if you are a young father or mother who wants to continue your studies, he may have a physical, emotional and overtime guess. It may mean asking a partner, friend or family member to take care of your child while they are studying. You may need to study at night and work during the day.

You can do this with your parents. Think about it because you can help yourself to cope with the daily pressure of caring for your baby. It means that it is used in a physical and physical context.

Education worth more than trying to see because it's has many benefits, including professional and financial security, to feed yourself and your baby.

CONCLUSSION

Years of research shows that the father-son dyad and the family environment; this includes all essential caregivers: they are the basis for the well-being and healthy development of children. Babies learn from birth and trust their parents and other caregivers in their lives to protect and care for them. The impact of parents cannot be higher than in the early years of a child's rapid brain development, and parents and the family environment create and shape almost all of their experiences. Parents help children develop and improve their knowledge and skills by establishing a path for their health and well-being in childhood and beyond. The fatherly experience also affects the parents themselves. For example, parents can enrich their parents' lives and focus on them. Create stress or relaxation; and a range of emotions including happiness, sadness, contentment and anger. Childhood parenting takes place today in the context of essential developments. It includes the rapid growth of early childhood science, which enables a more differentiated understanding of critical developmental stages and early childhood parents. With the increase in child poverty in recent years, funds for family programs and services have increased.

I hope after reading this short book, you will use permission to feel loved - how to parents help teens develop

Thank you for your interest in the final words, I hope you will rate me so that I will be more motivated to produce the best books for each reader.

Thank you.